Romeo and Juliet
The Hidden Astrological Keys

Great works of literature are like stars;
they stay put, even as we draw them
into new constellations.

—Adam Kirsch

Romeo and Juliet

The Hidden Astrological Keys

PRISCILLA COSTELLO, M.A.

ADAPTED FROM

Shakespeare and the Stars
The Hidden Astrological Keys to
Understanding the World's
Greatest Playwright

IBIS PRESS
Lake Worth, FL

Published in 2018 by Ibis Press
A division of Nicolas-Hays, Inc.
P. O. Box 540206
Lake Worth, FL 33454-0206
www.ibispress.net

Distributed to the trade by
Red Wheel/Weiser, LLC
65 Parker St. • Ste. 7
Newburyport, MA 01950
www.redwheelweiser.com

ISBN 978-0-89254-182-9
Ebook: ISBN 978-0-89254-649-7

Library of Congress Cataloging-in-Publication Data
Available upon request

Book design and production by STUDIO 31
www.studio31.com

Cover painting: the Cobbe portrait, ca. 1610
Smile retouch by Mimi Alonzo
Photo of Mercury by NASA
Cover design by STUDIO 31

Printed in the United States of America
[MG]

General Introduction:
Did Shakespeare Really Use
Astrological Symbols?

"It is the *stars*,/ The *stars* above us,
govern our conditions..." (*King Lear*)

"Methinks it should be now a huge
eclipse/ Of *sun* and *moon*..." (*Othello*)

"I know thy *constellation* is right apt
for this affair." (*Twelfth Night*)

Shakespeare's works are filled with references like these to heavenly bodies and stellar events. This isn't surprising since people of his time were more aware of the skies and the stars than we are: with no electric lights and few clocks, farmers, mariners, and the average Elizabethan looked to the sky to determine time and weather. Since personalities were classified in relation to specific planets (an early form of psychology) and medical practice was based on planetary types (or "temperaments"), the meanings of the astrological symbols were familiar to them.

For the illiterate (the majority) oral traditions passed down for generations made the astrological language familiar. The literate read yearly almanacs in English listing astrological omens. Educated Elizabethans grasped astrology's more profound implications since astrological language appeared frequently in religious writings. Steeped in the classical literature of ancient Greece and Rome, they knew that astrology is an integral part of an elegant, sophisticated, and intelligently-thought-out spiritual philosophy whose language and symbolism had been transmitted through the centuries and were part of lively discussion well into the 17th century (and still are today).

Like the members of Shakespeare's audience, his characters are also familiar with astrology.

His dramatis personae speak of stars, planets, comets, meteors, eclipses, planetary aspects, predominance, conjunction, opposition, retrogradation, and all sorts of astro-meteorology. They know that the Dragon's Tail exerts an evil influence, that Mercury governs lying and thievery, that Luna [the Moon] rules vagabonds and idle fellows, that Saturn is malignant and Jupiter benevolent, that the signs of the zodiac rule the limbs and organs of the body, that planets influence cities and nations . . . Although they do not go into details regarding the technical workings of the science, his characters on the whole seem to possess a general knowledge of stellar influence on human destiny. —Johnstone Parr[1]

---

1 Johnstone Parr, *Tamburlaine's Malady and Other Essays on Astrology in Elizabethan Drama*, U. of Alabama Press, 1953, p. 64.

We don't catch many of the astrological allusions in Shakespeare's plays and understand their significance because we're no longer steeped in the grand worldview that was fundamental to Elizabethan thinking. We're conditioned in our time by the dominant beliefs of conventional materialistic science: that only physical things are real and that the only way to acquire knowledge is through five-sense perception. But for hundreds of years before Shakespeare's time the dominant paradigm was of a universe unfolding from Divinity in an orderly progression of hierarchical levels, down through the realm of the fixed stars, through the "crystalline spheres" of the seven classical planets, and ultimately into the physical world of human beings, animals, plants, and minerals. The fact that the planets are an integral part of this worldview justifies looking at Shakespeare's plays through the lens of astrology.

Each level is linked with all the levels above and below it, so that references to the planets trigger a host of associations on all the other levels. In a worldview in which the heavens are reflected on Earth and the realm of Earth mirrors the heavens, it is natural to see a connection between the glorious Sun that dominates the skies and the King who is the focus of court and country. Shimmering moonlight is symbolically reflected in the sheen of silver. Because this worldview allows for sympathetic resonances between all levels of creation, Shakespeare can write of tempests both external to King Lear and within his mind, of eclipses that portend the fall of kings, and of horses that eat each other when Macbeth murders King Duncan. Events on one level of being can reflect events on another.

Since Shakespeare's works reflect this generally accepted worldview, the vast majority of his characters' statements are overwhelmingly in line with the Renaissance astrological worldview familiar to his audience. Shakespeare naturally draws on familiar astrological symbolism as creative inspiration for his art, in both obvious and subtle ways. He uses it for various purposes: to establish time and its passage; to create characters in line with planetary associations; and to allude to themes and philosophical ideas embedded in these symbols. Most of his plays focus on one particular sign of the zodiac and its associated ruling planet with the "key" of the piece being conveyed by the language and allusions in the first (or second) scene.

The following discussion of this particular play (books by the same author about other Shakespearean plays are also available) begins with a summary of the story, and then reveals the play's key: the zodiacal sign and its associated planet. The main part uncovers the connections between aspects of the play and relevant astrological symbols, considering their significance from different perspectives and on different levels. Important key words are CAPITALIZED to make it easy for readers to identify core ideas associated with the sign and planet.

Since the worldview of Shakespeare's time is so comprehensive, his allusions are wide-ranging, encompassing the heavenly spheres, the human world on all its levels, and the world of nature. My explorations are equally wide-ranging: they include the mythological, the psychological, the philosophical, the religious or spiritual, the esoteric, and of course the mundane (references to gems and minerals, plants and animals, weather conditions, and even separate parts of the human body that were all correlated with the heavens).

I hope that the resulting wide-ranging discussion will intrigue perceptive play-goers and eager readers of Shakespeare's works who wish to explore their hidden depths from a new and different perspective, one that provides fresh insights into Shakespeare's extraordinary creations. His "capacious" consciousness, combined with literary craft, midwived a unique body of work that could only have been produced at that particular time by an individual having an unusual combination of literary artistry, astute perception, and vivid imagination, along with a profound understanding of philosophical, esoteric, and spiritual wisdom—which includes astrology. It is this combination of gifts and talents that has made his works vital and intriguing for over four centuries.

And now on to .... *ROMEO AND JULIET*.

(The ideas here are condensed from the chapter entitled "The Hidden Astrological Key to *Romeo and Juliet*" in *Shakespeare and the Stars: the Hidden Astrological Keys to Understanding the World's Greatest Playwright* published by Ibis Press in 2016.)

Romeo and Juliet

Gemini and its Ruler Mercury

Here's much to do with hate, but more with love.
Why, then, O brawling love, O loving hate . . .

—(I, i, 168-9)

The Story

In Verona, Italy two equally noble families, the Montagues and the Capulets, clash, much to the displeasure of the town's Prince who threatens further fighting with a sentence of death. The lovesick Romeo, a Montague, who has been pining for Rosaline, is persuaded to go in disguise with friends to the Capulets' masked ball where, as fate arranges it, he meets Juliet, the Capulets' only daughter. They instantly fall in love. After the party Romeo sneaks into the Capulets' garden where he sees Juliet on her balcony, and they exchange lovers' vows. Romeo visits Friar Laurence, who agrees to marry them secretly, hoping to heal the two families' enmity.

Immediately after the wedding the angry Tybalt, Juliet's cousin, accosts some Montagues in the street and, trying to keep the peace, Romeo inadvertently allows Tybalt to stab his friend Mercutio to death. Enraged, Romeo fights and kills Tybalt. Instead of condemning him to death, the Prince exiles Romeo to Mantua. To distract the distraught Juliet (who's grieving for Romeo's banishment and not for Tybalt's death), her parents insist that she marry the Count Paris.

To help Juliet, Friar Laurence gives her an herbal concoction that will make her appear to be dead. The plan is that the Friar will send word to the banished Romeo so that he can rescue her from the family vault, and the two can then escape. But another messenger, who doesn't know of the ruse, reaches the exiled Romeo first. Romeo speeds to the tomb where he encounters and kills Paris, assumes that Juliet is dead, and swallows poison that he has obtained from an apothecary. Juliet awakes from the plant's spell, sees the dead Romeo, and stabs herself to death. The families, united in grief, vow a new peace.

The Sign Gemini and its Ruler Mercury

Shakespeare, the experienced dramatist, usually grabs the audience's attention in opening scenes by portraying violent acts or visitations from the supernatural (such as the appearance of the Ghost in scene 1 of *Hamlet* or the three Witches hovering over their cauldron at the opening of *Macbeth*). After such a dramatic opening, Shakespeare then introduces the main characters, gives some necessary back-story, and reveals through language and imagery the thematic basis of the drama.

So *Romeo and Juliet* is unusual in that the play begins with a Prologue that announces both the plot and the point of the story. In the form of a sonnet, a perfectly rhymed fourteen-line poem, the Prologue begins:

> *Two* households, both alike in dignity,
> In fair Verona, where we lay our scene,

From ancient grudge break to new mutiny,
Where civil blood makes civil hands
　　unclean.
From forth the fatal loins of these *two* foes
A *pair* of star-crossed lovers take their life;
Whose misadventur'd piteous overthrows
Doth with their death bury their parents'
　　strife.

So we know that we're in Italy (Verona) where Mediterranean passions run high and that the play will concern itself with TWO households "both alike in dignity", TWO lovers, and TWO foes, whose bitter hatred of each other has erupted again. Shakespeare strongly emphasizes both the equal status and the bitter opposition of the two enemy families. So when looking for a connection to zodiacal symbolism, we should look for a sign that is "double-figured", with two evenly balanced elements.

Only two signs have balanced doubles in them: Pisces, represented symbolically by two interlinked fish swimming in opposite directions, and Gemini, represented by twins or a glyph of two vertical lines connected by horizontal lines at the top and bottom. As we shall see, a multitude of points regarding language, characterization, and plot all point to the sign GEMINI as definitely providing the archetypal foundation of the play.

The symbol for the sign Gemini has TWO upright straight lines. The number two has great philosophical and metaphysical significance, for it holds the secret to

The symbol for the zodiacal sign Gemini has two upright lines, representing the multiple dualities that characterize the created world. These are either in balance or in conflict, with the potential also for each to turn into its opposite—day into night, summer into winter, peace into war—and back again. The lines at the top and bottom connecting the two pillars signify that the opposites are inextricably linked or contained in the One.

creation. For centuries the question was posed: How does creation happen? In ancient philosophy, the answer was that it begins with the One appearing to divide itself into two. The two multiply into numerous opposites that characterize the visible world and create our experience of it, with all its contrasted dualities: day and night, light and dark, male and female, and so on.

All these polarities desire either a balance, which holds the tension of the opposites in suspension, or a resolution back into unity or harmony. Unity is symbolized by the marriage of two human beings, or, on a grander scale, the marriage of heaven and earth. If neither happens, the opposites may wage war with each other. These ideas are embedded in the zodiacal sign of Gemini.

The polarity of two equal and opposed principles at war is reflected in the violent antipathy between the Montagues and Capulets, a necessary element of the dramatic story. Throughout the play, opposites are starkly contrasted: youth opposed to age, war to peace, happiness to despair, light to dark, and of course love to hate.

The play's connection to the sign Gemini is particularly revealed through the uniqueness of Shakespeare's language in this play. A special hallmark of *Romeo and Juliet* is the number of phrases containing diametrical OPPOSITES, known as "oxymorons" (from the Greek meaning "sharp-dull"), which combine contradictory words in one phrase. The antipathy between the two warring families is embedded in the play's very language! When Romeo first hears about the renewed clash between members of the two families in Verona's central square, he protests,

> Here's much to do with hate, but more with
>   love.
> Why then, O brawling love, O loving hate
>   . . .
> O heavy lightness! Serious vanity . . .
> Feather of lead, bright smoke, cold fire, sick
>   health,
> Still-waking sleep, that is not what it is!
>
> (I, i, 168-9, 171, 173-4)

Juliet speaks similarly. After meeting Romeo and falling in love with him, she hears from her Nurse who he really is. Shocked, Juliet complains,

> My only love sprung from my only hate!
> Too early seen unknown, and known too
>   late!
> Prodigious birth of love it is to me
> That I must love a loathed enemy.
>
> (I, v, 135-8)

Another balanced pair of opposites appears in Romeo and Juliet's families. Rarely in Shakespeare's dramas do we have both parents living and participating in the drama. In most of the plays we see single parents. In *A Midsummer Night's Dream*, for example, Hermia's father Egeus alone generates the conflict by insisting that his daughter Hermia marry Demetrius; there's no mother to soften his stubborn will. Yet in *Romeo and Juliet* Shakespeare gives us two equally balanced couples: Lord and Lady Montague, and Lord and Lady Capulet.

The play strongly emphasizes another important correlation with the sign Gemini. In the sequence of the zodiacal signs beginning with Aries and ending with Pisces, Gemini is the first of the AIR signs. The air element has to do with the mental or intellectual level of human beings and is associated with the development of the MIND and the subsequent ability to translate THOUGHTS into WORDS. Shakespeare's audience would have appreciated the fact that the positive manifestation of mental ability exhibited by the air sign Gemini is fluent and articulate speech. The downside is being GLIB, talkative without saying anything of substance, SUPERFICIAL, mentally busy but endlessly distracted, ingratiating but "phony"—and "mercurial" in the sense of being vacillating and undependable.

"Mercurial" Characters: Mercutio and the Nurse

To clinch the play's symbolic resonance with the sign Gemini, the planet associated with Gemini as its "ruler", Mercury, actually shows up as a character in the play! The name of one of the principal characters, Romeo's friend, is an obvious clue. "Mercutio" is the living embodiment of some facets of the symbolic Mercury, as would have been obvious to Shakespeare's audience. This short poem captures some of Mercury's recognizable qualities:

> Who's fond of life and jest and pleasure;
> Who vacillates and changes ever?
> Who loves attention without measure?
> Why, Gemini.[2]

This well describes Mercutio, whom we first meet the evening that Romeo and his friends go to the masked

---

2 Nicolas de Vore, *Encyclopedia of Astrology*, New York: Philosophical Library, 1947, p. 364.

ball at the Capulets' home. (Mercury loves disguises.) Mercutio is a talker, someone who loves to hear himself rattle on, a true child of Mercury. He reveals his gift of gab in a very long speech about the fairy queen Mab, triggered by Romeo's reference to a dream he had that night.

> O, then I see Queen Mab hath been with
>   you....
> She is the fairies' midwife, and she comes
> In shape no bigger than an agate stone
> On the fore-finger of an alderman,
> Drawn with a team of little atomi
> Athwart men's noses as they lie asleep.
> Her wagon spokes made of long spinners'
>   legs;
> The cover, of the wings of grasshoppers;
> Her traces, of the moonshine's wat'ry beams;
> Her collars, of the smallest spider web;
> Her whip, of cricket's bone, the lash of film;
> Her wagoner, a small grey-coated gnat
> Not half so big as a round little worm
> Pricked from the lazy finger of a maid.
> Her chariot is an empty hazelnut
> Made by the joiner squirrel or old grub,
> Time out o' mind the fairies' coachmakers.
> And in this state she gallops night by night
> Through lovers' brains, and then they dream
>   of love;

> O'er courtiers' knees, that dream on curtsies
>   straight;
> O'er ladies' lips, who straight on kisses
>   dream,
> Which oft the angry Mab with blisters
>   plagues
> Because their breath with sweetmeats
>   tainted are.
>
>   (I, iv, 53, 55-76)

Romeo interrupts this extended riff on Queen Mab (which goes on for forty lines!) with "Peace, peace, Mercutio, peace!/ *Thou talk'st of nothing.*" (I, iv, 95-6). Mercutio's improvisation is just for fun, which Romeo accurately perceives by saying his friend talks of "nothing." The Gemini type is known to be fond of inducing laughter through JOKES and WIT. Shakespeare's audience would immediately have recognized Mercutio as the type who runs off at the mouth at every opportunity and enjoys the joke himself.

Shakespeare also introduces a feminine version of Mercury in the person of another character who loves to talk. The female counterpart to Mercutio is Juliet's Nurse, whose first appearance on stage noticeably parallels Mercutio's. She dominates the scene in which Lady Capulet meets with Juliet to encourage her to marry her cousin, the "valiant Paris." Taking her cue from Lady Capulet's reference to Juliet's being of a "pretty" (that is marriageable) age, the Nurse reminisces garrulously about Juliet's weaning.

> I remember it well.
> 'Tis since the earthquake now eleven years,
> And she was weaned—I never shall forget
>   it—
> Of all the days of the year upon that day,
> For I had then laid wormwood to my dug,
> Sitting in the sun under the dovehouse wall.
> My lord and you were then at Mantua.
> Nay, I do bear a brain! ...
> And since that time it is eleven years,
> For then she could stand high-lone. Nay, by
>   th'rood,
> She could have run and waddled all about,
> For even the day before, she broke her brow,
> And then my husband—God be with his
>   soul,
> A was a merry man!—took up the child....
>
> (I, iii, 24–31, 37–42)

Lady Capulet breaks in, much as Romeo did, to bid the Nurse stop: "Enough of this. I pray thee, hold thy peace." The Nurse, however, enjoying the sound of her own voice (for thirty-three lines!), continues talking and repeats the joke. At that point even the young Juliet interrupts to stop her, saying, "And stint thou too, I pray thee, Nurse, say I." (I, iii, 51, 60) The Nurse is obviously another example of the connection the play has to the astrological symbolism of Gemini.

The Nurse's reminiscences are especially irritating because, unlike Mercutio's lines, hers are repetitive, true to the automatic nature of memory, as her mind recalls established associations she has with the incident she recounts. Her mind is clearly operating in mental ruts, in marked contrast to Mercutio's brilliant inventiveness. She and Mercutio illustrate yet another polarity, showing two different ways in which the mind can operate. Like Mercutio, though, she ends with the same sexual joke that he uses one scene later. When the toddler Juliet had fallen upon her face, the Nurse's husband had joked, "Thou wilt fall backward when thou hast more wit." (I, iii, 44) Mercutio's is a wittier and more educated version of the same joke because he makes a pun (a play on two meanings of the same word) when he speaks of the fairy queen Mab as one who "when maids lie on their backs,/ . . . presses them and learns them first to bear,/ Making them women of good carriage." (I, iv, 92-4)

So, significantly, we have TWO equally garrulous characters incarnating mercurial tendencies to run off at the mouth.

Mercutio and the Nurse actually meet later in the marketplace, when the Nurse is seeking Romeo. Here she fulfills a most important Mercurial function: being a GO-BETWEEN, in this case transmitting information between Juliet and Romeo. In classical mythology Mercury is the gods' messenger and with winged shoes and hat is capable of speedy travel between heaven and earth. This is Mercury's archetypal role: he is the gods' mouthpiece, a MESSENGER between gods and goddesses, between gods and human beings, or between one human being and another. In this case, Romeo tells the Nurse that Juliet is to go to Friar Laurence's cell that afternoon so that they may be married, happy news that she'll relay to Juliet.

Both Mercutio and the Nurse are comedians of a sort, providing comic relief in the drama. Mercutio relies more on witty and sophisticated word-play and the Nurse more on bawdy allusions. Each represents either the higher or lower type of mental functioning. To make this clear, Shakespeare has Mercutio speak most often in poetry while the Nurse speaks most often in prose. Mercutio's wit puts the Nurse at a disadvantage; when they meet in the street, Mercutio makes jokes at the Nurse's expense, singing a brief ditty that puns on "hoar" and "whore." (II, iii, 120-125) Shakespeare emphasizes Mercutio's qualities again when Romeo and the Nurse are at last alone, and the Nurse enquires as to Mercutio's identity:

> NURSE: I pray you, sir, what saucy merchant
>   was this that was so full of his ropery
>   [knavery]?
> ROMEO: A gentleman, Nurse, *that loves to*
>   *hear himself talk*, and will *speak more in a*
>   *minute* than he will stand to in a month.
>
>   (II, iii, 130-3)

Quick-witted to the end, Mercutio jests even as he is dying, stabbed by Tybalt's sword that passed under Romeo's arm. How many can make a pun as they bleed to death: "Ask for me tomorrow, and you shall find me a *grave* man"? (III, i, 93-4) Significantly, an ill-aspected Mercury in a horoscope can synchronize with poor hand-arm coordination or mistimed and erratic action that fails to achieve its goal.

Those who exhibit the qualities of Mercury are known to be "mercurial" or changeable. This quality is characteristic of the Nurse who is CAPRICIOUS. For a good part of the play it seems that the Nurse has Juliet's best interest at heart. She even warns Romeo against trifling with her lady's heart:

> . . . if ye should lead her in a fool's para-
> dise, as they say, it were a very gross kind of
> behaviour, as they say, for the gentlewoman
> is young; and therefore if you should *deal*
> *double* with her, truly it were an ill thing to
> be offered to any gentlewoman, and very
> weak dealing.
>
> (II, iii, 147-52)

Yet ironically it is the Nurse herself who later "double deals" (the idea of DOUBLENESS again, associated with Gemini). When Juliet begs her advice after her parents demand that she marry Paris, the Nurse ignores the fact that Juliet is already married to Romeo. She reasons that "Romeo is banished, and all the world to nothing/. . .

Then, since the case so stands as now it doth,/ I think it best you married with the County./ O, he's a lovely gentleman!/ Romeo's a dishclout to him." (III, v, 212-13, 216-19)[3] Seeing that the situation has dramatically changed and that events warrant adapting to new circumstances, the Nurse, conscience-free (like Mercury, whose actions—like stealing Apollo's cattle immediately after his birth—are often morally suspect), easily changes sides, even counseling Juliet to become a bigamist! (Note that a bigamist is a person who marries TWO people.)

> Ancient damnation! O most wicked fiend!
> Is it more sin to wish me thus forsworn,
> Or to dispraise my lord with that same
>   tongue
> Which she hath praised him with above
>   compare
> So many thousand times? Go, counsellor!
> Thou and my bosom henceforth shall be
>   *twain.*
>
>   (III, v, 235-40)

("Twain"—notice the allusion to twoness or division again.)

Like the Nurse, Romeo too seems FICKLE at the beginning of the play, going on and on about Rosaline

---

3 To impress Juliet with the County Paris' worth, she compares him to an eagle, the king of birds which is at the highest level within the avian kingdom.

whom he says he loves. But his elaborate protestations of love sound more intellectual than emotional. At this point Romeo is clearly more fixated on the *idea* of being in love than he is actually *feeling* love. This is consistent with Gemini's reputation for INCONSTANCY and for talking about emotions rather than experiencing them.

In fact, the Gemini personality may prefer to avoid messy emotions altogether in favor of intellectual gamesmanship. Mercutio, the incarnation of Mercury, certainly recommends this. After exchanging witty banter with Romeo (when he seems to be over his infatuation with Rosaline), Mercutio delightedly advocates mental interchange over emotional turmoil: "Why, is not this better now than groaning for love? Now art thou sociable, now art thou Romeo, now art thou what thou art by art as well as by nature, for this drivelling love is like a great natural [idiot] . . ." (II, iii, 76-9)

The Language of the Young Lovers

When Romeo truly falls in love with Juliet, we see a sharp contrast between his superficial preoccupation with Rosaline and his genuinely passionate and intense feelings for Juliet. No wonder, though, that Romeo's friends, seeing such a sudden change, doubt his sincerity. So how do we, the audience, privileged to witness Romeo and Juliet's first encounter, know that the instant mutual recognition of love between them has a completely different quality than Romeo's lovesickness for Rosaline? How do we know that the resolution of the warring opposites may occur through their coming together? We know because the lines they exchange upon first meeting create a perfect sonnet, each line effortlessly following the previous one in the required rhyme and number of lines. The poetry reveals the meeting not just of their lips but of their souls.

> ROMEO: [*To Juliet, touching her hand*]
>   If I profane with my unworthiest hand
>   This holy shrine, the gentler sin is this:
>   My lips, two blushing pilgrims, ready
>   stand
>   To smooth that rough touch with a
>   tender kiss.
> JULIET: Good pilgrim, you do wrong your
>   hand too much,
>   Which mannerly devotion shows in this.
>   For saints have hands that pilgrims'
>   hands do touch,
>   And palm to palm is holy palmers' kiss.
> ROMEO: Have not saints lips, and holy
>   palmers, too?
> JULIET: Ay, pilgrim, lips that they must use
>   in prayer.
> ROMEO: O, then, dear saint, let lips do what
>   hands do:
>   They pray; grant thou, lest faith turn to
>   despair.

JULIET: Saints do not move, though grant for
      prayers' sake.
ROMEO: Then move not while my prayer's
      effect I take.
[He kisses her]

                         (I, v, 90-104)

In an astonishingly short time, Romeo moves from greeting to hand-touching to kissing!—typical of speedy Mercury.

What signals the transformation from immature young people to mature courageous lovers is the expressive heights to which their interchanges rise. "Coming back to the effects of love on the two main characters, the most dramatic change is in their command of LANGUAGE," remarks Northrop Frye, one of the twentieth-century's most respected literary critics.[4] Romeo's earlier speeches were self-indulgently rhetorical (like Mercury showing off), well illustrated by these rather forced rhymed lines in which he complains of Rosaline's cool aloofness:

BENVOLIO: Then she hath sworn that she will
      still live chaste?
ROMEO: She hath, and in that sparing makes
      huge waste;
      For beauty starved with her severity
      Cuts beauty off from all posterity.

---

4 *Northrop Frye on Shakespeare*, Ed. Robert Sandler, Markham, Ontario: Fitzhenry & Whiteside, 1986, p. 24. [Emphasis added].

She is too fair, too wise, wisely too fair,
To merit bliss by making me despair.
She hath forsworn to love, and in that
vow
Do I live dead, that live to tell it now.

(I, i, 210-17)

(An actor delivering these lines would do well to sound pompous and self-consciously "poetic.") But once he meets Juliet and is driven to lurk unseen in the Capulets' garden hoping to see her, Romeo's language soars:

She speaks.
O, speak again, bright angel; for thou art
As glorious to this night, being o'er my head,
As is a *winged messenger of heaven*
Unto the white upturned wond'ring eyes
Of mortals that fall back to gaze on him
When he bestrides the lazy-passing clouds
And sails upon the bosom of the air.

(II, i, 67-74)

Romeo imagines Juliet here as a variant of Mercury, an angelic carrier of messages between mortals and the gods and thus a bridge-being.

Juliet too evolves from the obedient daughter who says practically nothing in her first appearance on stage other than to acknowledge her mother's authority.

JULIET: How now, who calls?

NURSE: Your mother.

JULIET: Madam, I am here. What is your will?

(I, iii, 5-7)

As the drama unfolds, fueled by passion, she speaks much more and speaks more eloquently, rising to poetic heights as when she appeals to the sun to set sooner so that Romeo may come to her bed:

Gallop apace, you fiery-footed steeds,
Towards Phoebus' lodging. Such a waggoner
As Phaethon would whip you to the west
And bring in cloudy night immediately.
Spread thy close curtain, love-performing
    night,
That runaways' eyes may wink, and Romeo
Leap to these arms untalked of and unseen!

(III, ii, 1-7)

The Sign Opposite to Gemini: Sagittarius

Shakespeare often, and more subtly, includes an opposite in another way: he indirectly references the sign that is opposite to the dominant sign for that play. This is the sign that is directly across from it on the zodiacal wheel. In *Romeo and Juliet*, Friar Laurence is the embodiment of the sign Sagittarius, opposite to Gemini and ruled by

Jupiter. As psychologist C. G. Jung might have explained, as soon as you have emphasis on one end of a polarity, you automatically constellate its opposite. The opposite is always present, but unseen until it is called into conscious awareness by the stress on the other end of the polarity.

As the opposite and complementary sign to Gemini, Sagittarius represents the higher mind in contrast to the lower or mercurial one. While Gemini focuses on information that is of immediate use but often ephemeral, Sagittarius embraces broader knowledge that has longer term validity and has stood the test of time. Such knowledge has accumulated and been systematized over many hundreds of years. This includes such studies as history, philosophy, religion, metaphysics, and education.

The good friar well embodies many of these associations. He is a member of a religious order, and as such is presumed to be an embodiment of wisdom. The advice he gives at different points in the narrative is both wise and rational. The tragic ending of this play results in part from the lovers' impetuousness, as they rush headlong into love and then into a secret marriage. Friar Laurence, religious advisor to both, admonishes them to "love moderately," to go "wisely and slow. They stumble that run fast"—good advice when trying to restrain Mercury's impulsiveness. (II, ii, 94)

In addition, he is an herbalist. This marks him as a carrier of the ancient wisdom tradition.

Herbalism or the Doctrine of Signatures

[H]e that would know the operation of the Herbs
must look up high as the Stars, astrologically . . .
—Nicholas Culpeper, *The Complete Herbal*

The use of plants and herbs for healing derives from the conceptual model still current in Shakespeare's time, which sees connections between humanity and nature. According to the old traditions, nature provides a cure for every human ill, because the human and natural worlds are part of a greater whole and are resonantly connected.

Herbalism is the science of using the esoteric properties of plants in both medicine and magic. Plant remedies are chosen according to the doctrine of correspondences or sympathies. Plants' virtues are recognized by their "signatures," revealed in their appearance or their taste, all in line with astrological symbolism. Their outward appearances offer clues to their inner properties, and consequently their uses:

A Martial plant is dry and hot, fiery even; a Saturnine plant is dank and cool, perhaps poisonous (though in right doses, poisons can be healing too); a Venusian plant is warm and moist, perhaps softly furred; a Solar plant is golden, probably follows the sun during the day (as does the sunflower), and is good for strengthening the human being; a lunar plant is cool and dry, good perhaps for women's ailments—and so forth. Each plant bears the signature of planetary virtues or qualities, and by these do we know immediately its uses or meanings.⁵

Shakespeare's audience would have been familiar with these associations of planetary qualities with earthly plants. Friar Lawrence, apparently an expert in herbalism (and therefore in astrology), offers an eloquent summary of the philosophy underlying the use of nature's medicinal offerings.

> I must up-fill this osier cage of ours
> With baleful weeds and precious-juiced
>   flowers.
> The earth, that's nature's mother, is her tomb.
> What is her burying grave, that is her womb,
> And from her womb children of divers kind
> We sucking on her natural bosom find,
> Many for many virtues excellent,
> None but for some, and yet all different.
> O mickle is the powerful grace that lies

---

5 Arthur Versluis, *Shakespeare the Magus*, Grail Publishing, St. Paul: MN, 2001, p. 42. On the same page Versluis also quotes from the famous Renaissance herbalist Nicholas Culpeper's classic *The Complete Herball*, a portion of which was cited at the beginning of this section: "I knew these various affections of man, in respect of sickness and health, were caused naturally . . . by the various operations of the Microcosm . . . as the cause is, so must the cure be; and therefore he that would know the operation of the Herbs, must look up high as the Stars, astrologically . . . ." Emphasis added. See all of Chapter IV, "The Sacred Lore of Plants."

In plants, herbs, stones, and their true qual-
    ities,
For naught so vile that on the earth doth live
But to the earth some special good doth
    give;
Nor aught so good but, strained from that
    fair use,
Revolts from true birth, stumbling on abuse.
Virtue itself turns vice being misapplied,
And vice sometime's by action dignified.

                              (II, ii, 7–22)

Friar Laurence is such an adept in this art that he seems almost an arbiter of life and death. The potion he concocts to help Juliet escape the unwanted (second) marriage and join Romeo in Mantua will make her appear dead, though she will only be asleep. In line with the astrological symbolism of Gemini, which embraces opposites, the Friar's harmless concoction contrasts to the poison sold to Romeo by the apothecary, an altogether less ethical character than the good friar.

Friar Laurence's last words in the above quotation point to one of the more profound ideas inherent in the symbolism of Gemini. The friar stresses the opposition of weeds and flowers, of earth as both womb and tomb, and of the potential of even the most healing preparation to be harmful or poisonous. This alludes again to the endless polarities of the visible world: day and night, male and female, good and evil. In the visible world things can easily flip into their opposites in ironic reversals ("Virtue itself turns vice being misapplied / And vice sometime's by action dignified"), because the underlying (and esoteric) truth inherent in the sign Gemini is that behind all polarities must be an all-inclusive, undifferentiated One. Ultimately both Romeo's and Juliet's loathing of each other's family is dissolved by their instant liking, and so too the hatred of Capulet for Montague and Montague for Capulet transmutes to love by the end of the play.

The dualities of Gemini are reflected in a modern description of its symbol from an astrological text: the two upright lines are equivalent to "the two temple columns as symbol of the day and night side, as the division of unity, as the differentiation into subject and object, masculine and feminine, the conscious and unconscious, light and dark, heaven and earth, etc."[6] The idea of two pillars fronting a temple is a very ancient one:

> Pillars representing the male and female principles were to be found at temples throughout the East. They were not incorporated in the structure but stood in front of the entrance, the columns forming a symbolic gateway, or door of life.... The two pillars, Jachin

---

6 This pictograph also symbolizes the "dual character of the creative forces which were thought to be responsible for life on earth." Banzhaf, Hajo, and Anna Haebler. *Key Words for Astrology.* York Beach, ME: Samuel Weiser, Inc., 1996, p. 28.

and Boaz, which stood before the temple of Solomon, had male and female names."[7]

This same duality characterizes the inner world of the individual as well as the outer world of form, as Friar Laurence cautions:

> Two such opposed kings encamp them still
> In man as well as herbs—grace and rude
>   will;
> And where the worser is predominant,
> Full soon the canker death eats up that
>   plant.

> (II, ii, 27–30)

Since poetic language is open-ended and allows for more than one interpretation, the Friar may have in mind a number of inner dualities as the "opposed kings" he refers to: the higher self versus the lower self, one's good angel versus the voice of the tempter, or reason versus passion (a frequent theme in Shakespeare's works).

The Flaw that Generates the Tragedy: Impulsiveness

Juliet's impatient urging of the Sun to set faster than normal points to a Gemini trait that characterizes the entire tragic story. We are told in the Prologue that the

---

7 Ernest Busenbark, *Symbols, Sex, and the Stars In Popular Beliefs*, Escondido, California: The Book Tree, 1997, p. 202.

*The Apothecary Shop. Apothecaries, forerunners of modern phar-
macists, mixed and sold a variety of items, especially medicinal
preparations made from herbs as well as organic (human and
animal) and inorganic substances. Apothecaries also sold sweets
(sugar being thought to have medicinal properties) and, particularly in Italy, ground pigments for artists' use.*

*Traditional knowledge of healing with herbs, passed down
orally from ancient times, was preserved in monasteries and nun-
neries during the Middle Ages (so Friar Laurence is appropriately
a member of a religious order), but into the Renaissance apothecary shops became independent dispensers of preparations and so
freed from church oversight. The more unscrupulous purveyors,
like the one Romeo seeks out in Mantua, sold poisons.*

"star-cross'd lovers" will die at the end, so we know in advance that the play is a tragedy. For Shakespeare's audience, a tragic outcome implied that the characters have some responsibility for this. This idea goes back at least to ancient Greece where Aristotle suggested in his *Poetics* that doomed heroes had a "tragic flaw" and that this personal flaw was the chief reason for their downfall. For the Elizabethans, these flaws related to the characters' temperament, which revealed the excesses and imbalances of their personalities. So significant were these imbalances that both human beings and fictional creations might suffer—even die—as a result of them.

In *Romeo and Juliet* the character flaw is obviously IMPULSIVENESS, the tendency to act before thinking or to act out of impulse or desire without examining the consequences. This is an exaggerated manifestation of the planetary ruler of Gemini, Mercury. Positively, Mercury is deemed capable of speedy flight, quick movement, and deft eye-hand coordination, but negatively, when actions are sudden and thoughtless or speed accelerates beyond reasonable limits, the consequences are likely to be unsuccessful outcomes or, at an extreme, life-threatening accidents.

We see this impulsiveness repeatedly in the characters' impatience and their hasty actions.

Even the love-struck Juliet, despite being carried away by emotion, seems to grasp intuitively the wisdom of Friar Laurence's advice: love moderately and take things more slowly. Early in the play, leaning from her balcony as she and Romeo exchange vows of love, she presciently worries:

> Although I joy in thee,
> I have no joy of this contract tonight.
> It is too rash, too unadvised, too sudden,
> Too like the lightning which doth cease to
> be
> Ere one can say it lightens.
>
> (II, i, 158-62)

Yet later, awaiting the slow Nurse's return from her mission to meet with Romeo, she succumbs to impatience:

> Love's heralds should be thoughts,
> Which ten times faster glide than the sun's
> beams
> Driving back shadows over louring hills.
> Therefore do nimble-pinioned doves draw
> Love,
> And therefore hath the wind-swift Cupid
> wings.
> Now is the sun upon the highmost hill
> Of this day's journey, and from nine till
> twelve
> Is three long hours, yet she is not come.
> Had she affections and warm youthful blood,
> She would be as swift in motion as a ball.

My words would bandy her to my sweet
 love,
And his to me.
But old folks, many feign as they were
 dead—
Unwieldy, slow, heavy and pale as lead.

(II, iv, 4-17)

How much faster are the young than the old! How much faster are thoughts, the products of mercurial activity, than the slow actions of time and time-bound creatures!

In the philosophical model of the time, reason was exalted as the guiding influence within the human being and was seen as a reflection of the Divine. To ignore its influence could generate increasingly unpleasant, even disastrous, consequences. In case the passionate young people missed his earlier counsel, Friar Lawrence repeats his advice to moderate passion when Romeo and Juliet arrive at his cell to be married. Despite his willingness to unite them in hopes of creating harmony between the two warring families, he cautions them again (and fore-shadows the tragic end to the story):

These violent delights have violent ends,
And in their triumph die like fire and pow-
 der,
Which as they kiss consume. The sweetest
 honey

Is loathsome in his own deliciousness,
And in the taste confounds the appetite.
Therefore love moderately. Long love doth
    so.
Too swift arrives as tardy as too slow.

(II, v, 9-15)

Once you grasp the connection between the characters' precipitous actions and the archetypal Gemini/Mercury, correlations leap out from almost every speech. Juliet later voices her excited impatience while awaiting the secret night-time visit of Romeo, the first they will spend as a married couple before he must leave, exiled to Mantua. And she does so in words that both reflect her desire for the speedy arrival of night and describe the opposites inherent in Romeo himself (in italics):

Come night, come, Romeo; come, *thou day
    in night,*
For thou wilt lie upon the wings of night
Whiter than new snow on a raven's back.
Come, gentle night; come, *loving, black-
    browed* night,
Give me my Romeo . . .
So tedious is this day
As is the night before some festival
To an impatient child that hath new robes
And may not wear them.

(III, ii, 117-21, 28-31)

Characters are constantly urging each other to speak or to act more quickly. The overwrought Juliet invokes an early coming of night and Romeo. The next morning her father issues excited instructions to the servants before the expected nuptials of Juliet and Paris:

> CAPULET: Come, stir, stir, stir! The second
>   cock hath crowed.
> The curfew bell hath rung. 'Tis three o'clock.
>   . . .
> Make haste, make haste. Sirrah, fetch drier
>   logs.
> Call Peter. He will show thee where they are.
>   . . .
> The County will be here with music straight,
> For so he said he would. I hear him near.
> Nurse! Wife! What ho, what, Nurse, I say!
> Go waken Juliet. Go and trim her up.
> I'll go and chat with Paris. Hie, make haste,
> Make haste, the bridegroom he is come
>   already.
> Make haste, I say.
>   (IV, iv, 3-4, 14-6, 21-7)

Right after this speech the apparently-dead Juliet is discovered and celebration turns instantly to mourning. Consistent with the mercurial nature of the play, the tone changes immediately to its opposite:

CAPULET: All things that we ordained
   festival
Turn from their office to black funeral.
Our instruments to melancholy bells,
Our wedding cheer to a sad burial feast,
Our solemn hymns to sullen dirges change;
Our bridal flowers serve for a buried corpse,
And *all things change them to the contrary.*

(IV, iv, 111-17)

The Idea of Twin Souls and Love at First Sight

The sign Gemini is often represented visually by the figure of TWINS. Doubles appear in myth, religious iconography, and legend as (among other pairs) the twin brothers Castor and Pollux (one mortal and the other divine), as the siblings Isis and Osiris (who were also husband and wife), and as Tristan and Iseult/Isolde (unrelated and fated lovers)—and now the literary characters Romeo and Juliet.

The idea of twins and twin souls, a concept that explains love at first sight, first appears in Plato's accounts of Socrates' philosophical teaching in ancient Athens (dating from the 5th c. BCE). In one of his dialogues, the *Symposium*, guests at a supper party deliver speeches on the subject of love. One of them, Aristophanes, declares that in the beginning there was a third type of human being, not either male or female but both male <u>and</u> female, hermaphrodites descended from the Moon.

Since in their strength, energy, and arrogance they tried to scale the heights of heaven and attack the gods, Zeus split them in two. This not only made them weaker, but also

> . . . left each half with a desperate yearning for the other, and they ran together and flung their arms around each other's necks, and asked for nothing better than to be rolled into one. . . . So you see . . . how far back we can trace our innate love for one another, and how this love is always trying to redintegrate our former nature, *to make two into one*, and to bridge the gulf between one human being and another.
>
> . . . we are all like pieces of the coins that children break in half for keepsakes—*making two out of one*, like the flatfish—and each of us is forever seeking the half that will tally with himself. [8]

Despite their youth, the instant attraction between Romeo and Juliet is not an attraction between body and body, but soul and soul. Romeo intuits that Juliet is his soul-self when he declares "It is my soul that calls upon my name./ How silver-sweet sound lovers' tongues by night,/ Like softest music to attending ears!" (II, i, 209-11) The concept of a soul is found in almost all cultures and all religions. In the West, the idea of an immaterial aspect of a human being conjoined with a material

---

8 *The Collected Dialogues of Plato, Symposium*, pp. 543, 544, sections 191a, 191d, 191e. Emphasis added.

body during physical life and separated from it at death appears at least as far back as ancient Egypt as well as in Plato's writings in ancient Greece.

This individual soul is thought to be the organ of spiritual perception, a hidden faculty of super-sensing and intuitive knowing. This faculty responds not to the ups and downs of human emotions, but to a higher octave of feeling: the rapture of experiencing higher dimensions, even the Divine. The closest many of us might get to experiencing this, while we are still embodied and relatively unawakened, is the exaltation we feel when attending religious services or when exposed to great art. This individual soul is thought to retain the wisdom of distilled experience, which carries over into the next life.

Although Romeo and Juliet recognize the soul-filled and hence inevitable nature of their attraction, the rest of the characters in the play (with the exception of Friar Lawrence and the Nurse) are completely unaware of their developing relationship. Romeo's friends in particular are quite in the dark. Juliet acknowledges the deep connection she has with Romeo soon after meeting him at the ball. In the famous "balcony scene" Romeo overhears her musing on what constitutes a person's true identity. She is looking beyond his mundane identity to his very essence:

> O Romeo, Romeo, wherefore art thou
> Romeo?
> Deny thy father and refuse thy name . . .
> 'Tis but thy name that is my enemy.

Thou art thyself, though not a Montague.
What's Montague? It is nor hand, nor foot,
Nor arm, nor face, nor any other part
Belonging to a man. O be some other name!
What's in a name? That which we call a rose
By any other word would smell as sweet.
So Romeo would, were he not Romeo called
...   (II, i, 74-6, 80-7)

Juliet's ponderings reflect a long-standing philosophical debate about language. Philosophers and linguists ask, "Do the words we use to identify things actually reflect the essence of those things? Is it even possible for words to represent the reality of a person or object? Or are they just labels, perhaps contradicting the inner essence?"

We're back to themes associated with Gemini here, about thoughts, words, and language. Glib mercurial types like Mercutio and the Nurse can supply names or labels for everything but often miss the essential meaning. The inner essence of a person or thing exists beyond the outer appearance, distinct from personality or character. It's the unrecognized perfection of Being, the true inner Self.

Both Romeo and Juliet use phrases that reflect their mutual recognition of this glorious essence, beyond labels and beyond even physical reality. For Romeo, Juliet is "the sun", the source of light and life, thought in modern astrology to be indicative of your core self. Even though

Romeo comprehends how dangerous it will be to trespass in Capulet's orchard, he must do so: "Can I go forward when my *heart* is here?/ Turn back, dull earth, and find thy *center* out." (II, i, 1-2) "Heart" and "center" are both code words for this essence. One of the indications of a soul-based relationship is this very recognition of the beauty of the other's soul, with the innate understanding that one is recognizing one's own Self.

Individuation and Initiation in Romeo and Juliet

The ancient Greeks said that love ennobles us. A modern psychologist might say that it individuates us—that is, we become more authentically who we are, separate from our parents and capable of acting autonomously, according to our own will and in our own best interests. The youthful Romeo mooning over Rosaline or blubbering on the floor of Friar Laurence's cell evolves into a man who takes direct action in hastening to Verona, fighting with Paris, and dying for love. The immature Juliet, who assured her mother that she would warm to Paris only as far as her mother gave consent, becomes the independent and fearless woman who dares to take Friar Laurence's potion and, like Romeo, to die for love. Psychologically, Romeo and Juliet have "individuated."

Modern psychologists, particularly followers of C. G. Jung, have suggested that aspects of psychological transformation are like aspects of ancient initiatory ceremonies conducted by groups devoted to spiritual pursuits.

Such ceremonies developed, it seems, because thoughtful Greeks were dissatisfied with the unseemly antics of Greek gods like Zeus (Jupiter in Rome), busy seducing mortal women and evading his jealous wife. The twelve gods and goddesses who lived on Mount Olympus seemed more like glorified human beings than dignified divinities. Educated Greeks turned to other paths. Both Pythagoras and Plato were reputed to be members of private religio-philosophic schools found in Egypt and elsewhere around the Mediterranean Sea and called "Mysteries." While these groups offered public festivals and open rituals during the day for any adherent, they are better known for the private and closed initiations often celebrated at night.

While these mystery schools operated independently of the state-sanctioned religion, they were well known and accepted in the culture of their day. Dedicated to various deities, both local and imported from abroad— Orpheus in Greece, or Demeter and her daughter Persephone at Eleusis, or Isis and Osiris from Egypt—the secret ceremonies these groups conducted were rituals voluntarily undergone, more personal than the public religious ceremonies, and designed to transform the participant by a direct experience of the sacred.

We still don't know precisely what occurred in their initiation rites, for, astonishingly, over hundreds of years (between the 6th c. BCE and almost 400 CE when imperial decrees prohibited what were by then described as "pagan cults") not a single initiate out of thousands ever divulged the whole of what transpired. A few dropped tantalizing hints: Plato, for one, was severely criticized for revealing some of the secret philosophic principles in his writings.

We do know that an allegorical drama with profound spiritual import was performed for the assembled initiates, a reminder that theater then was not only esteemed as high art but was originally presented in honor of the gods and goddesses—that is, it had primarily a religious function. Are we surprised that the plays of Shakespeare have imbedded in them some of the same philosophic ideas?

Most of the Mystery schools imparted some special teachings reserved for initiates or those preparing for initiation. In particular,

[T]he Mysteries were devoted to instructing man concerning the operation of divine law in the terrestrial sphere. Few of the early cults actually worshiped anthropomorphic deities, although their symbolism might lead one to believe they did. They were moralistic rather than religionistic; philosophic rather than theologic. They taught man to use his faculties more intelligently, to be patient in the face of adversity, to be courageous when confronted by danger, to be true in the midst of temptation, and, most of all, to view a worthy life as the most acceptable sacrifice to God, and his body as an altar sacred to the Deity. [9]

---

9 Manly P. Hall, *The Secret Teachings of All Ages: an Encyclopedic Outline of Masonic, Hermetic, Qabbalistic and Rosicrucian Symbolical Phi-*

Watching what happens to Macbeth or Lear is certainly a dramatized lesson about the consequences of one's moral choices in light of a grander philosophic worldview.

Many of the mystery schools not only existed as underground fraternities but also staged their initiations literally underground in caves or structures created beneath the earth. One of the first spiritual heroes, the ancient Persian sage Zarathustra, was said to have initiated his followers in underground caverns hidden in the forests. In several of Shakespeare's plays, like *A Midsummer's Night's Dream* and *As You Like It*, the protagonists escape to a forest where they are in some way transformed.

So there's great significance in the setting of the final stage of *Romeo and Juliet*: a burial crypt, full of decomposing bodies of dead Capulets. From what we know of the later Greek mystery schools, initiations were designed especially to confront the participant with his greatest fear: the fear of death. Tellingly, Mercury was in Greek myth not only the messenger between heaven and earth, but also the divinity who guided the dead to and from the underworld.

Shakespeare foreshadows the tragedy and magnifies the threat of death in order to heighten the lovers' heroism and to stress the similarity of their experience to an

---

losophy, Los Angeles, CA: The Philosophical Research Society, Inc., 1978, p. xxi.

initiation. Juliet is caught in a bind: her father demands
that she marry Paris, yet she's already married to Romeo.
She goes to Friar Laurence's cell distraught, threatening
to kill herself. He suggests that she can escape physical
death if she goes along with his "remedy": a double strat-
agem that involves her taking a potion that gives only the
appearance of death and Romeo rescuing her from the
moldy tomb when she wakens. But the good Friar warns
that she will still (as in the ancient initiatory rites) have
an encounter with Death himself.

> If, rather than to marry County Paris,
> Thou hast the strength of will to slay thyself,
> Then is it likely thou wilt undertake
> *A thing like death* to chide away this shame,
> *That cop'st with Death himself to scape from it;*
> And, if thou dar'st, I'll give thee remedy.
>
> (IV, i, 71-6)

Juliet vows that love will give her the strength to
meet whatever initiatory trials she fears, all described as
confrontations with death in one form or another:

> O, bid me leap, rather than marry Paris,
> From off the battlements of any tower,
> Or walk in thievish ways, or bid me lurk
> Where serpents are. Chain me with roaring
>   bears,
> Or hide me nightly in a charnel house,

O'ercovered quite with dead men's rattling
    bones,
With reeky shanks and yellow chapless
    skulls;
Or bid me go into a new-made grave
And hide me with a dead man in his
    tomb—
Things that, to hear them told, have made
    me tremble—
And I will do it without fear or doubt,
To live an unstained wife to my sweet love.

                      (IV, i, 77-88)

The lovers' final encounter is in a cave-like place. When Romeo comes to the churchyard on this fatal night, he must *go down* into the vault where Juliet's body lies. He instructs his servant Balthasar to "stand all aloof,/ And do not interrupt me in my course. Why I *descend* into this *bed of death/* Is partly to behold my lady's face . . ." (V, iii, 26-9)

We're prepared for the final scene in the archetypal underworld by the lovers' own premonitions. The very last time that Juliet sees the living Romeo, as he is leaving her bed to flee to Mantua to endure his banishment, she has a disturbing vision:

O God, I have an ill-divining soul!
Methinks I see thee, now thou art so low,
As one dead in the bottom of a tomb.

Either my eyesight fails, or thou look'st pale.

(III, v, 54-7)

Her physical eyesight hasn't failed but has been superseded by "second sight", as she foresees the future, the final act of the drama. Romeo too has a prescient vision: "I dreamt my lady came and found me dead—/ Strange dream, that gives a dead man leave to think!" Yet Romeo's dream of death has a transcendent finale, for in it Juliet "breathed such life with kisses in my lips/ That I revived and was an emperor." (V, i, 6-9)

Their Final Union and The Mystic Marriage

The astrological sign Gemini contains within it both the mystery of creation, the emergence of two out of One, and its completion, when through the union of two there is a return to the One. The most common image for this is a wedding. This may be the deeper reason that comedies typically end with at least one wedding. With two becoming one symbolically, harmony and unity are restored.

Some of these ideas are found in esoteric tradition, divided into the Lesser and Greater Mysteries. The Lesser Mysteries help you to manage your life successfully in this world, and are symbolized by the physical marriage of a bride and bridegroom (and the sexual secrets accompanying it). The Greater Mysteries prepare you for the transcendent experience of the human soul's joining with the Soul of the World, the Anima Mundi. This conscious union of human and divine is also universally envisioned as a wedding, though on a grander scale. A wedding, whether on a microcosmic or macrocosmic scale, is

> . . . an almost universal symbol for the uniting of polar opposites . . . which from that point on function no longer antagonistically or competitively but complementarily, forming together a higher unity, a whole that is more than the sum of the parts. For the ancients, the *hieros gamos* ("sacred wedding") was a symbol for the creative uniting of heaven and earth, male and female, god and goddess . . . [10]

No wonder that weddings are such charged events, carrying not only the weight of the emotions of the bride and groom, the expectations of the parents, and society's hopes for the continuation of life, but also the deeper symbolism of the resolution of opposites—the Lesser and Greater Mysteries conflated into one celebration.

> Traditional symbols of love always express a duality in which the two antagonistic elements are, nevertheless, reconciled. . . . They are, in other words, symbols of a conjunction, or the expression of the ultimate goal of true love: the elimination of dualism and separation,

---

10 Hans Biedermann, *Dictionary of Symbolism: Cultural Icons and the Meanings Behind Them*, NY, NY: Penguin Books, 1994, pp. 216-7.

uniting them in the mystic 'centre', the 'unvarying mean' of Far Eastern philosophy. The rose, the lotus flower, the heart, the irradiating point—these are the most frequent symbols of this hidden centre; 'hidden' because it does not exist in space, although it is imagined as doing so, but denotes the state achieved through the elimination of separation. The biological act of love itself expresses this desire to die in the object of the desire, to dissolve in that which is already dissolved.[11]

The Ultimate Tragedy

Romeo and Juliet not only complete the "biological act of love", but they also ultimately die, as foretold in the Prologue. We can lay much of the blame for the final tragedy on factors related to Mercury. Consistent with a poorly-functioning (in astrological terms, a badly-aspected) Mercury, MISCOMMUNICATION abounds in the play. In every case, events appear to be fated. IF ONLY Capulet's *illiterate* servant had not happened to meet Romeo and Benvolio in the street and asked them to *read* the party invitation for him; IF ONLY Benvolio had not urged Romeo to go to the Capulets' party as a distraction from his mooning over Rosaline; IF ONLY Juliet's parents had not decided at the most critical time to arrange a marriage for Juliet (who was already secretly married

---

11 J. E. Cirlot, *A Dictionary of Symbols*, NY, NY: Philosophical Library, 1962, p. 185.

to Romeo); IF ONLY Friar Laurence's *letter* had reached Romeo in Mantua so that he would know that Juliet's appearance of death was false... All of these contribute to the tragic outcome and all seem dramatically necessary, for only with the ultimate sacrifice that both Romeo and Juliet make, to die for love, will the enmity between the two households die too.

Terrible sacrifices are frequently enacted in tragedies. Noted literary critic Northrop Frye makes some cogent observations about these tragic gestures:

> Romeo and Juliet are sacrificial victims, and the ancient rule about sacrifice was that the victim had to be perfect and without blemish. The core of reality in this was the sense that nothing perfect or without blemish can stay that way in this world, and should be offered up to another world before it deteriorates. That principle belongs to a still larger one: nothing that breaks through the barriers of ordinary experience can remain in the world of ordinary experience. One of the first things Romeo says of Juliet is: "Beauty too rich for use, for earth too dear!"[12]

Romeo and Juliet operates on several levels: it's a human tragedy, an acutely observed psychological drama, and a vehicle for spiritual truths. The human tragedy is that youth and beauty are sacrificed to the hardened

---

12 Northrop Frye, *Northrop Frye on Shakespeare*, p. 32.

demands of a city-consciousness that has divided itself into TWO heart-hardened enemy camps. But a psychological transformation has taken place in both of the lovers, as they struggle with their passions, confront their fears, and mature into young adults. And a spiritual transformation appears to take place at the end of the play as the warring opposites fuse and become one.

The Prince of Verona chastises both the Montagues and Capulets when he says, "See what a scourge is laid upon your hate,/ That Heaven finds means to kill your joys with love. . . . All are punished." (V, iii, 292-3) Old Capulet, Juliet's father, begs his former enemy, "O brother Montague, give me thy hand," and the gesture of hand-clasping signals the resolution of the conflict of opposites that has driven the conflict between the two families.

Old Montague, Romeo's father, generously offers to raise a statue of Juliet in pure gold. In honoring the daughter of his former enemy and especially in creating a likeness of her in the most valued of all metals, a higher level of peace and harmony is invoked. That remarkable proposal is echoed by Capulet, who offers to raise one "as rich" of Romeo to lie by Juliet's. For each of them dies not just for the other, but for Love. The extraordinary self-sacrifice of the two young people has in effect transubstantiated them from flesh to golden Light. The duality of Gemini, so prevalent in the manifest world with its ever-present clashing opposites, is resolved into a spiritual unity. With this acknowledgement and in sad recognition of the foolishness of their quarrel, all the characters make their exit as the onlookers contemplate the tragic exaltation of the two "star-cross'd lovers."

ADDENDUM

A Word on the Dominant Key to
All Shakespeare's Romantic Comedies: Venus

> All tragedies are finish'd by a death,
> All comedies are ended by a marriage.
> —George Gordon, Lord Byron (Don Juan, Canto 3)

Shakespeare wrote three types of plays: comedies, tragedies, and histories. Although individual plays may be keyed to different zodiacal signs and their ruling planets, *all* of the comedies and *all* of the tragedies have one dominant and consistent symbol: Venus for the former and Mars for the latter.

While the dating of his plays is an ongoing matter of debate, it is fairly well established that Shakespeare's first plays—probably *The Comedy of Errors* and *The Two Gentlemen of Verona*—were comedies. In all his comic plays Shakespeare is clearly drawing on conventions of comedy widely known in his time, due in part to the revival of classical literature in the Renaissance.

From a literary perspective, comedy evolved from ancient Greek performances that in turn evolved from fertility rituals marking the renewal of life after a period of quiescence or apparent death. Comedies commonly end with marriages, a pre-eminent symbol of rebirth, announcing a change in the protagonists' identities and promising the eventual birth of new beings. They thus celebrate the triumph of life over death, analogous to warm spring overcoming cold winter.

All of Shakespeare's comedies provide pleasure and feature ROMANCE—especially romantic involvement leading to at least one wedding. The archetypal VENUS is always associated with the comedies, either primarily or secondarily, since she symbolizes the powerful attraction between people that leads to their bonding both privately and publicly and so to the creation of new life. As the principal symbol for comedy, Venus is on one level the type of love that ideally leads to marriage: the private union of two happy people and the public celebration reassuring society that the family and the social order will continue.

Shakespeare's comedies follow the comic pattern developed in Roman times, featuring plots about various obstacles in the way of such lovers uniting and being allowed to marry. Many literary critics, like the brilliant Northrop Frye, remark on this:

> At the core of most Renaissance comedy including Shakespeare's, is the formula transmitted by the New Comedy pattern of Plautus and Terence. The normal

action is the effort of a young man to get possession of a young woman who is kept from him by various social barriers: her low birth, his minority or shortage of funds, parental opposition, the prior claims of a rival. These are eventually circumvented, and the comedy ends at a point when a new society is crystallized, usually by the marriage or betrothal of hero and heroine. The birth of the new society is symbolized by a closing festive scene featuring a wedding, a banquet, or a dance.[13]

Shakespeare knows this tradition. Since "the course of true love never did run smooth," in *A Midsummer Night's Dream* he has Lysander and Hermia deliver a list of all the obstacles that can delay the joining of the young man and the young woman (all useful plot devices to the playmaker of comedies).

> LYSANDER: But either it was different in
> blood—
> HERMIA: O cross!—too high to be
> enthralled to low.
> LYSANDER: Or else misgraffed in respect of
> years—
> HERMIA: O spite!—too old to be engaged to
> young.

---

13 Northrop Frye, *A Natural Perspective: The Development of Shakespearean Comedy and Romance*, New York: Harcourt, Brace & World, Inc., 1965, p. 72.

LYSANDER: Or merit stood upon the choice
    of friends—

HERMIA: O hell!—to choose love by anoth
    er's eyes.

LYSANDER: Or if there were a sympathy in
    choice,

    War, death, or sickness did lay siege to it,
    Making it momentary as a sound,
    Swift as a shadow, short as any dream ...

                    (I, i, 134–44)

Each of Shakespeare's romantic comedies focuses on a different type of love and in some cases a different obstacle. *A Midsummer Night's Dream* and *Romeo and Juliet* focus on youthful and exuberant love, while *Much Ado About Nothing* features mature lovers. What keeps the older Beatrice and Benedick apart is not an external obstacle but an internal factor: their own cynical and sharpened wit arising from overdeveloped intellects which lead them to attack each other verbally. In other words, they are too much in their heads and not enough in their hearts. (Or too much Mercury and not enough Venus!)

In *A Midsummer Night's Dream,* though, the lovers do face an external obstacle: the parental opposition of Hermia's father. He objects partly because he thinks that Lysander has bewitched the naïve Hermia by the usual ploys of Venus—rhymes, nosegays, and sweetmeats among them. Egeus believes that his daughter is too young and inexperienced to recognize true love. And *A Midsummer Night's Dream* is a certainly about superficial love, typical of youth and particularly subject to fluctuating tides of emotion and changes in circumstances.

The young lovers featured in that play—Hermia and Lysander and Helena and Demetrius—are not especially individualized characters. They could be *any* young lovers. No surprise that their feelings are easily and comically transferred from one object of love to another during their time in the forest. Whether we accept that a flower's juice alters their affections or that it is a symbol of shallow emotional attachments thought to be characteristic of the young, first Lysander and then Demetrius switch the objects of their affections with stunning speed. Venus has a hand in this. Oberon explicitly attributes the power of the flower's juice to her son Cupid (and so indirectly to her) and asserts that whomever the lover sees when he wakes, she will "shine as gloriously / As the Venus of the sky." (III, ii, 106–7)

Obstructive parents lurk in *Romeo and Juliet* and *The Merchant of Venice*, too. Old Capulet insists on Juliet marrying Paris despite her protests and threatens to throw her out onto the streets if she does not comply. Portia's dead father has imposed a strange test on any suitor for her hand: choosing between three caskets of gold, silver, and lead. Although she finds this frustrating, in the end it works to her advantage as only her preferred suitor

Bassanio passes the test. But in *The Tempest* a powerful father is not an obstacle but the principal arranger of the happy union of his daughter Miranda with the princely Ferdinand. We can be assured of the attunement of their souls because they (like Romeo and Juliet) recognize and fall in love with each other at first sight.

Despite the erratic trajectory of the lovers' relationships in all of Shakespeare's comedies, we are happy to see that in the end, as Puck promises, "Jack shall have Jill, / Naught shall go ill, / the man shall have his mare again, and all shall be well." (III, iii, 45–7)

Shakespeare and the Stars
The Hidden Astrological Keys to Understanding the World's Greatest Playwright

Priscilla Costello, M.A.

- A unique interpretation of six of Shakespeare's best-known plays in light of astrological symbolism
- Explains the deep influences of astrology in the spiritual and philosophical worldview of Shakespeare's time
- Shows how the archetypes of astrology are the models for Shakespeare's vivid characters and the rationale for his language and imagery
- Draws on fundamental ideas of Western philosophy, mythology, religion, and esoteric wisdom as well as modern psychology

The first half of this unique and groundbreaking work provides necessary background for understanding Shakespeare's plays by describing the synthesis of both classical and Christian ideas of his time.

The second half examines six of Shakespeare's best-loved plays in the light of astrological symbolism, mythology, and modern depth psychology.

Thoroughly researched and well-illustrated, this book is a clear and brilliant synthesis that challenges conventional literary criticism of Shakespeare's works. By grounding its analysis in verifiable historical information, modern readers will find that this book illuminates the plays from a fresh perspective that deepens and profoundly transforms their understanding of them.

Please visit *PriscillaCostello.com* and
ShakespeareandtheStars.com for more information

Literature, Astrology, Psychology
528 pp. • 6 x 9 Paperback•Illustrations • $29.95
ISBN: 978-0-89254-216-1 • Ebook: 978-0-89254-631-2

Shakespeare and the Stars
Playbill Editions
Priscilla Costello, M.A.

These six small books are 64 pages each and printed in a convenient trim size. They can be taken to theater performances or studied before and after reading or seeing a play.

These books celebrate the 400th anniversary of Shakespeare's death and offer fresh and exciting insights into the ever-popular works of the world's greatest playwright. Each analysis specifically highlights Shakespeare's use of the archetypal language of astrological symbolism in both obvious and subtle ways. Such references would have been well known in Shakespeare's time, but their deeper significance is lost to modern-day playgoers and readers.

The most unique aspect of these books is the revelation that many of Shakespeare's plays are entirely keyed to a specific zodiacal sign and its associated (or ruling) planet. Shakespeare's audience would have immediately grasped their significance in revealing character, foreshadowing the plot, and establishing key themes for each play.

The Merchant of Venice
ISBN: 978-0-89254-175-1
Ebook: 978-0-89254-642-8

The Tempest
ISBN: 978-0-89254-178-2
Ebook 978-0-89254-644-2

King Lear
ISBN: 978-0-89254-176-8
Ebook: 978-0-89254-643-5

Romeo and Juliet
ISBN: 978-0-89254-182-9
Ebook 978-0-89254-649-7

A Midsummer Night's Dream
ISBN: 978-0-89254-181-2
Ebook: 978-0-89254-648-0

Macbeth
ISBN: 978-0-89254-177-5
Ebook 978-0-89254-646-6

Each book is $11.00 • Paperback • 64 pp. • 5 ½ x 8 ½

Priscilla Costello, M.A., Dipl. CAAE, is an educator, writer, speaker, and counseling astrologer. An enthusiastic lover of Shakespeare's work, she taught English language and literature for over 30 years. As a professional astrologer, she has the unique ability to synthesize Shakespeare's literary and astrological themes. Her double prize-winning M.A. thesis focused on religious philosophy and Jungian psychology. Founder and Director of The New Alexandria, a center for religious, spiritual, and esoteric studies, she is the author of *The Weiser Concise Guide to Practical Astrology* (2008) and *Shakespeare and the Stars: The Hidden Astrological Keys to Understanding the World's Greatest Playwright* (2016).

Please visit *PriscillaCostello.com* and *ShakespeareandtheStars.com* for more information